DRUGS AND THEIR DANGERS

MARIJUANA AND ITS DANGERS

by Kari A. Cornell

BrightPoint Press

San Diego, CA

BrightPoint Press

© 2020 BrightPoint Press
An imprint of ReferencePoint Press, Inc.
Printed in the United States

For more information, contact:
BrightPoint Press
PO Box 27779
San Diego, CA 92198
www.BrightPointPress.com

LIBRARY OF CONGRESS CATALOGING-IN-PUBLICATION DATA

Names: Cornell, Kari A., author.
Title: Marijuana and its dangers / by Kari Cornell.
Description: San Diego, CA : ReferencePoint Press, [2020] | Series: Drugs and
    their dangers | Audience: Grades 9-12. | Includes bibliographical
    references and index.
Identifiers: LCCN 2019000787 (print) | LCCN 2019002570 (ebook) | ISBN
    9781682827109 (ebook) | ISBN 9781682827093 (hardcover)
Subjects: LCSH: Marijuana abuse--Juvenile literature. | Marijuana
    abuse--Prevention--Juvenile literature. | Marijuana--Juvenile literature.
Classification: LCC HV5822.M3 (ebook) | LCC HV5822.M3 C6685 2020 (print) |
    DDC 362.29/5--dc23
LC record available at https://lccn.loc.gov/2019000787

CONTENTS

FACT SHEET

- Almost half of users smoke marijuana daily or almost daily.

- One in six teens that use it daily will become addicted.

- As of 2019, thirty-three states and Washington, DC, had legalized marijuana in some way.

- Since the early 2000s, the number of people who are addicted has doubled.

- Marijuana is made from the dried flowers, stems, leaves, and seeds of the cannabis plant.

- Regular users are more likely to experience depression and anxiety.

- Marijuana smoke contains 50 to 75 percent more carcinogens (chemicals that cause cancer) than tobacco smoke.

- Cannabidiol (CBD), a chemical in marijuana, has been shown to prevent seizures, ease pain, help people sleep, increase appetite, and calm anxiety.

- Dropping out of favorite activities to smoke marijuana is a sign of addiction.

- Half of people who enter treatment for marijuana addiction are under twenty-five years old.

THE FIRST TIME

Anyone who has smoked marijuana has a story. Many of these stories begin the same way. People try the drug as teenagers. Many think it's not a big deal. They may think it is something harmless and fun.

Many people try an illegal drug for the first time as teenagers. This can have many negative effects on a young person's life.

One teen says,

The first time I smoked weed was

during the summer before eighth

Marijuana use may start casually, but it can become addictive. It can take over a person's life.

grade. I was really curious to see

what it was all about. I had a few hits

but didn't really get stoned. Later, I

smoked some more. I got so high I

didn't even know what was going on.

The next chance I got to get high, I

jumped on it. The more I did it, the

more I liked it.[1]

"My love of pot started the first time I

got stoned. I was fourteen," another teen

says.[2] "The first time I smoked pot I didn't

see the point, because I didn't feel high. I'd

been drinking for a year already and I liked

alcohol. The first time I did feel stoned from

weed, I dropped the bottle and picked up

the pipe."[3] That teen also says that the two

years before getting sober were terrible.

The teen could act sober in order not to

get caught. But the teen's parents still knew what was happening. Eventually the teen was arrested for dealing marijuana. After that the teen was also arrested for shoplifting.

Some people use marijuana once in a while. But others start using the drug more and more. At first a person might think using marijuana is fun. Later they may feel the need to smoke it every day. And as is the case for many, smoking marijuana may also lead to other negative behaviors. For some, this can be shoplifting or dealing drugs.

Using drugs can lead to dealing drugs and other bad activities.

CHAPTER ONE

WHAT IS MARIJUANA, AND HOW IS IT MADE?

Marijuana is also known as cannabis. It has many casual nicknames too. It is called pot, weed, and grass. The drug comes from two plants. They are *Cannabis sativa* and *Cannabis indica*. Cannabis plants come from

Marijuana plants are grown all over the world. They can be identified by their leaves.

Central Asia. They were used as medicine. Cannabis has grown in China for over six thousand years. Since then, marijuana has been grown all over the world. It has spread to Europe and the Americas.

The plant contains many chemicals. There are two important ones. THC affects the mind. It makes users feel a high. The second is CBD. It does not make the user high. Instead, some researchers believe CBD has medical uses. It is believed to

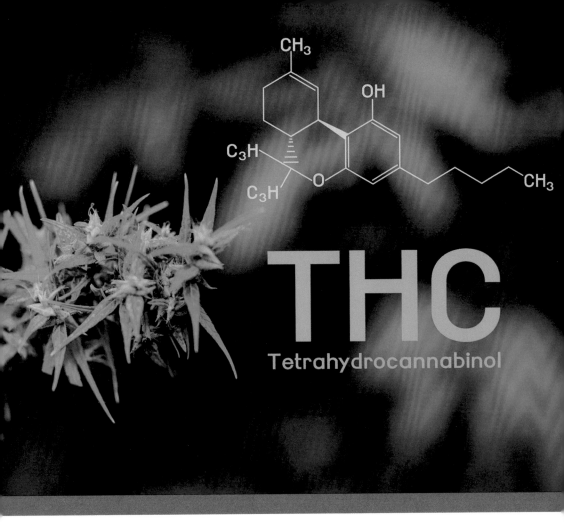

CH₃

OH

C₃H

C₃H

O

CH₃

THC
Tetrahydrocannabinol

THC is the most well-known chemical in marijuana.
It provides most of the effects of taking marijuana.

ease pain. Different kinds of marijuana have

different amounts of THC and CBD.

The United States started making laws

about marijuana in 1937. It passed the

One of the most common ways to use marijuana is to smoke it. This can be done with a joint, blunt, pipe, or several other ways.

Marihuana Tax Act. The name of the drug is sometimes spelled with an *h* instead of a *j*. The act taxed sellers of marijuana. Originally, the American Medical Association opposed the act.

The act passed one year after "Reefer Madness" swept the country. People heard stories of violent marijuana users. The stories said criminals had superhuman strength. Marijuana had come to the United States from Mexico. This meant many of the stories were connected to immigrants. The stories were made up to scare people. The government made new laws. Eventually marijuana was illegal throughout the United States.

As of March 2019, thirty-three states and Washington, DC, had legalized marijuana. Some allowed only medical use. Others let people use it for any reason. Other states were considering legalizing it as well. Marijuana has become more accepted. Legalizing the drug may suggest it is harmless. But this is not true, especially for kids. It can be harmful for growing brains. For teens, marijuana can be damaging. Professor of psychiatry Patricia Conrad says, "Cannabis causes cognitive impairment and delayed cognitive development in adolescents."[4] Scientists are still learning how it affects the human body.

HOW IS MARIJUANA CONSUMED?

Marijuana is made from cannabis flowers, stems, leaves, and seeds. These parts are shredded and dried. Then users smoke them. They can be rolled up in papers to make cigarettes. These are called joints. Blunts are hollowed-out cigars filled with marijuana. Users may also stuff the leaves into a pipe. Drug dealers may add addictive drugs to marijuana. These can include heroin or phencyclidine (PCP). Users don't always know what they are getting.

There are other ways to use marijuana besides smoking. The leaves and flowers may also be soaked in butter. That butter can be baked into foods. These baked goods are called edibles. Marijuana can be brewed as a tea. Cannabis oil can be

Marijuana can be added to baked goods. These edibles are part of a growing marijuana industry.

Marijuana and marijuana extracts can be added to teas, other drinks, and foods.

inhaled using a vaporizer or smoking pipe.

These same oils can be used to make

sprays or waxes. They are also added to

foods, candies, or drinks. Using cannabis oil

is called dabbing. No matter how marijuana

is taken, it enters the bloodstream. Once

the THC reaches the brain, it begins to

affect the user.

CHAPTER TWO

WHAT IS THE DRUG'S EFFECT ON THE BODY?

Marijuana enters the bloodstream at different rates. It depends on how it is consumed. When inhaled, the effects happen quickly. The smoke enters the lungs. Tiny air sacs called alveoli line the lungs. This is where THC passes into the

Inhaling marijuana is the fastest way for it to enter the bloodstream.

bloodstream. The blood carries the drug to

the brain.

Users can feel a wide range of effects from marijuana. It can make them happy, anxious, or even hungry.

THC levels are lower if marijuana is eaten. The effects are delayed. It takes up to an hour for the effects to start. The drug must first make its way to the stomach. It is broken down there. Then it can be absorbed into the blood. Blood carries THC to the brain. The effects last longer than if the drug is inhaled.

As THC floods the brain, some users feel relaxed and happy. The drug changes the senses. It can change the user's sense of time. It can make people laugh. It may make them hungry. Others become anxious and panicked. Some may hallucinate. They see things that aren't really there. To understand these effects, it helps to know how the brain works. THC interferes with brain function.

HOW THE BRAIN WORKS

Nerve cells carry messages around the body. They also communicate within the brain. Nerve cells in the brain are called neurons. They deliver messages to parts of the brain.

Chemicals called neurotransmitters move messages between neurons. A neurotransmitter leaves one neuron. It connects to a matching receptor on another neuron. It carries a message. The brain

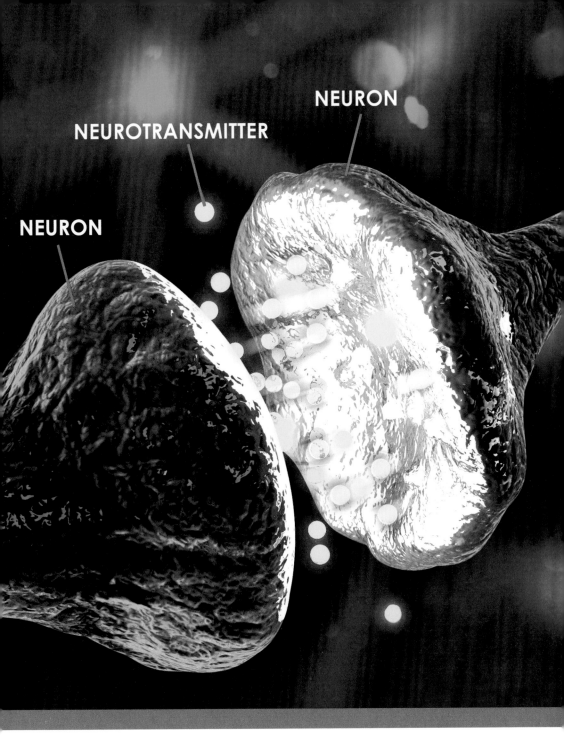

NEURON

NEUROTRANSMITTER

NEURON

Neurotransmitters send messages between neurons. THC interferes with this process.

sends this message to the body. Different neurotransmitters carry different messages.

HOW DOES MARIJUANA AFFECT THE BRAIN?

THC attaches to cannabinoid receptors. The receptors exist naturally. They are found in several parts of the brain. These parts include the hippocampus, cerebellum, and hypothalamus. Anandamide is a chemical produced in the brain. It usually binds with cannabinoid receptors. When THC blocks these receptors, anandamide cannot do its job. This keeps the brain from working correctly.

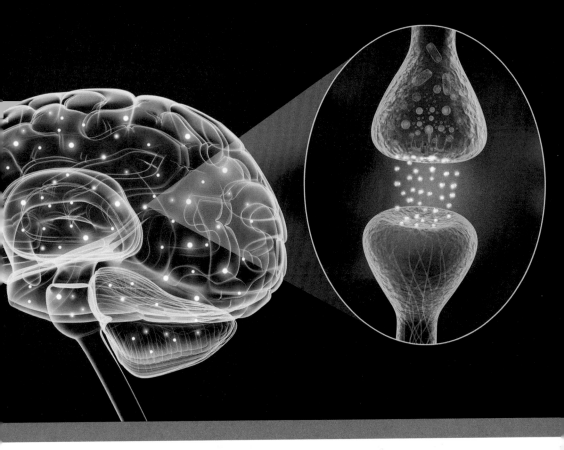

THC affects receptors all over the brain.

THC scrambles the way the brain works. The hippocampus controls short-term memories. This is why users may have a poor memory. The cerebellum helps control coordination. This is why a user becomes clumsy. The hypothalamus normally controls

EFFECTS ON THE BRAIN

Neuroscientist Judith Grisel says, "By flooding the entire brain, as opposed to select synapses, marijuana can make everything . . . take on a sparkling transcendence." Marijuana use hurts the ability to enjoy normal experiences. This is bad timing for teens. They are just starting to make important life decisions.

Judith Grisel, "Pot Holes: Legalizing Marijuana Is Fine. But Don't Ignore the Science on Its Dangers," Washington Post, May 25, 2018. www.washingtonpost.com.

appetite. This is why a user becomes hungry. Cannabinoid receptors are also in the neocortex. This area controls complex thinking. THC binds with receptors there. This negatively affects judgment. It also alters a person's sense of time.

Frequent marijuana use can affect brain function. This can hurt schoolwork and other parts of life as well.

LONG-TERM EFFECTS OF MARIJUANA USE ON THE BRAIN

THC affects body and brain functions for days. Using marijuana on the weekend can affect time at school. Memory and problem solving are key to learning. Marijuana use affects these skills. This makes it more difficult to learn. Teens' brains are still developing. This makes the effects even more harmful.

In teens who use marijuana frequently, effects can be long term. Studies show

SCHOOL AND POT DON'T MIX

Marijuana has a negative impact on learning. Among twelfth graders, 6.5 percent report that they use it daily or almost daily. And 22.7 percent report having used the drug in the past month. High schoolers who use marijuana regularly are more likely to drop out.

that marijuana changes some pathways in the brain. These pathways are linked to higher-thinking functions. One New Zealand study linked drops in IQ scores to teen marijuana use.

When teens start using marijuana, their grades often fall. There are many reasons. One reason is marijuana's effects on the brain. Teens may also start other behaviors that affect grades. They may see school as less important. Some users deal drugs. Others shoplift. These behaviors lead to arrests. An arrest can harm a teen's grades. They may miss class for hearings.

They could have to switch schools. They might even go to juvenile detention.

MARIJUANA AND MENTAL ILLNESS

Scientists have noted a connection between marijuana use and mental illness. Those who use it regularly are more likely to experience depression and anxiety. But it is hard to know if marijuana is the cause. Researchers wonder if people with these illnesses are drawn to marijuana.

Heavy marijuana use can worsen certain mental illnesses. The age at which a teen first tries marijuana can affect this

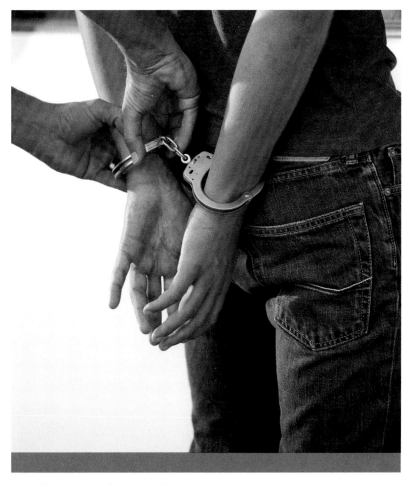

Marijuana is illegal in many places. Users can be arrested.

connection. So can the amount used and

the body's response to it.

INCREASED RISK FOR CANCER AND OTHER DISEASES

Smoking marijuana can cause the same diseases cigarette smokers face. In fact, smoking pot can be worse. Marijuana smoke contains 50 to 75 percent more cancer-causing chemicals. Researchers found that teen marijuana users are at higher risk for a rare type of testicular cancer. The risk is doubled.

The American Lung Association says, "Research shows that smoking marijuana causes chronic **bronchitis**."[5]

Smoking can affect the lungs. Smokers of any kind often have a cough from breathing smoke.

Driving while high is dangerous. In many places it carries the same sentence as driving while drunk.

It can make users more likely to get

respiratory infections.

Marijuana use can also increase the risk

for heart disease. It can cause wider social

problems, too. People who drive while high can cause car accidents. Users who drop out of school may struggle to find good jobs. When these things happen, society pays a price.

CHAPTER THREE

HOW DOES MARIJUANA USE AFFECT PEOPLE'S LIVES?

Many people believe marijuana is not addictive. Some states have legalized the drug. Young people may think it is harmless. However, marijuana can be addictive and dangerous. Judith Grisel is a scientist. She studies the brain. She

Some people march to support legalizing marijuana.

says, "The brain adapts to marijuana as it does to all abused drugs, and these neural adjustments lead to tolerance, dependence and craving—the hallmarks of **addiction**."[6]

THE SYMPTOMS OF ADDICTION

People who become addicted crave the drug. They begin to use more of it. Users may have trouble sleeping. They might become angry. They may feel sick. They may not want to do anything other than smoking pot. They try to quit but can't.

These symptoms affect the user's life. The user becomes dependent. They use marijuana just to feel normal. They need it to get through the day.

SIGNS OF POSSIBLE ADDICTION

There are warning signs of addiction. One is not being able to quit. On average, adults

Many users may have trouble sleeping or feel anxious. This is one of the signs of marijuana addiction.

who seek treatment have tried to quit six

times. With addiction comes tolerance. The

brain gets used to THC over time. More

of the drug is needed for the same effect.

THC changes how the user experiences life. The user adjusts to this feeling. Everyday activities may become boring without getting high. Users spend more time getting the drug. They ignore problems it creates. Problems may include getting suspended at school. A user may drop out of their favorite activities.

Finally, users who try to quit have withdrawal symptoms. These happen when they go without marijuana. These can include shakiness and headaches. The user may also have chills, sweating, or fever.

Using marijuana can make everyday events seem boring. The users often want to get high instead of performing necessary tasks.

Symptoms go away once the user takes more marijuana.

AN INCREASE IN ADDICTIONS

More teenagers smoke pot than cigarettes. A 2018 study looked at high school seniors. It found that 30 to 40 percent

Addiction centers can help users through their withdrawal and learn ways to stay clean.

smoked marijuana in the past year. About

20 percent used it in the past month. And

6 percent smoked daily. In 2016, four

million people over the age of twelve had a

marijuana use disorder.

Drug addiction can lead to poor choices in the user's life. These choices can affect schoolwork and jobs now and in the future.

The number of high school seniors using

marijuana is going up. So is the number

of people seeking help. This may be due

to the stronger marijuana today. Teens

are starting to use it at younger ages than

in the 2000s. These numbers point to a

rising problem.

FEDERAL STATUS

Marijuana is still illegal by federal law. New

state laws do not change this. Some states

have made marijuana legal. Local police will

not arrest a person for having marijuana.

But federal authorities can still arrest

them. Some states that have legalized the

drug have freed some people in jail for marijuana-related crimes.

HOW DOES ONE PERSON'S ADDICTION TO MARIJUANA HAVE AN IMPACT ON SOCIETY?

Marijuana addiction affects all parts of a person's life. Eventually, this affects a community. Teens who begin using marijuana early are more likely to develop an addiction.

Teens who use marijuana often are more likely to be absent from school. Missing school affects schoolwork. A marijuana user's grades may drop. Depression and

Students who miss class to smoke or sell marijuana can get in trouble.

lack of motivation are linked to marijuana

use too. Together, these factors could make

a struggling student drop out. Job options

are limited for people without high school

STRESS AND MARIJUANA

Stress puts people at a higher risk for getting sick. Stress wears the immune system down. With a weakened immune system, the body cannot fight off illnesses. For users, the chances of getting bronchitis and pneumonia rise even higher.

diplomas. The jobs that are available have low pay. They might not include paid time off. They may not provide health insurance.

If a person in this situation gets sick and misses work, pay is even lower. Dips in income can be devastating. He or she may not have savings. The user may be unable

Certain side effects of marijuana can lead to getting sick. Calling in sick to work can cause income loss.

to pay for rent or food. Many people are just

one paycheck away from being homeless.

People in this situation depend on

help. This could be from state and local

government programs. They may need

government health care. If they are addicted

to marijuana, they may need community

drug treatment programs. Society uses

taxes to pay for these services. The costs of

marijuana use can affect the whole society.

If users miss too much work, they could lose their jobs. In extreme circumstances, they could even become homeless.

CHAPTER FOUR

HOW CAN PEOPLE QUIT USING MARIJUANA?

T reatment is different for everyone. What works for one person may not work for another. There is no approved medication for marijuana withdrawal. But there are other options. Marijuana Anonymous is a support group. People who want to

For many people with addictions, support groups are key to getting help. Different formats of therapy work better for different people.

quit go to one of these groups. They talk

about their struggles. There are other

support groups too. Users can also attend

counseling programs. They get advice from

experts. Half of users in treatment are under twenty-five. Those who seek help are trying to live a healthier life.

THERAPY FOR MARIJUANA USE DISORDER

Therapists suggest ways to change a person's behavior. This can help the person avoid drug use. This is called behavioral treatment. There are three different types. The first is motivational enhancement therapy. The second is cognitive-behavioral therapy. The third is contingency management. The treatments usually work best together.

Therapy teaches people with addictions ways to say no to drugs and stay clean. With the right tools, they can be successful.

In motivational enhancement therapy, the user talks about how they feel. The therapist focuses on the decision to quit. The therapist and patient set goals.

DRUGS TO TREAT MARIJUANA USE DISORDER

No drugs are available to treat marijuana use disorder. But research is in progress. One approach is to treat the symptoms. For some, taking a sleeping medication helps. Others use medications for anxiety or stress.

They make plans to achieve them. They talk through pros and cons. They work through the challenges of changing. Cognitive-behavioral therapy teaches skills to cope with cravings. This helps the person build good habits. These habits allow them to quit. Contingency management rewards patients for quitting. They are tested twice a week. If the test is negative, they get a voucher. Its value increases with each drug-free test. Vouchers can be traded in for healthy items or services.

SCHEDULE 1

Society remains divided on marijuana use. It is classified as a Schedule 1 drug under the Controlled Substances Act. Schedule 1 is the most restricted drug category. Schedule 1 drugs can easily be abused. The government says they have no medical uses. However, a 2018 poll showed

CBD medications are often prescribed to help prevent certain kinds of seizures.

that 63 percent of Americans favored legalizing marijuana.

The CBD in marijuana has shown promising medical results. It has been used to help many people sleep. It can ease pain. Other chemicals in marijuana may help boost the body's ability to fight some illnesses. They may also protect the brain after traumatic events. But few studies have been done with these chemicals. Marijuana's status as a Schedule 1 drug makes it hard to get. This makes doing medical research difficult.

WOULD DECRIMINALIZING MARIJUANA HELP?

There are different opinions on **decriminalizing** marijuana. Decriminalization means that penalties are reduced for marijuana-related crimes. It is often still illegal. But state governments would not strongly enforce these laws.

Some argue that relaxing laws would lead to more teen marijuana use. But the opposite might be true. In the United States, drug laws are stricter than in other countries. Yet US teens are more likely to use marijuana. A 2016 study found

Decriminalization supporters say that changing marijuana laws would lower the number of people in jail for nonviolent crime.

RACIAL PROFILING AND MARIJUANA

Some believe that marijuana laws unfairly affect people of color. Most affected are African American men. This was seen in New York City between 2015 and 2018. Black people were eight times more likely to be arrested for minor marijuana charges than white people.

31 percent of US tenth graders have used marijuana. The study found that only 16 percent of European tenth graders used it. In some states, marijuana is now legal. But marijuana use has not gone up in these places.

LEGALIZATION PROCESS

Changes to marijuana's status require new laws. States that wish to change marijuana laws must follow a process. A state proposal is put to a vote. The citizens of that state have to vote on whether they want to legalize marijuana. They may decriminalize it. They may make it legal for medical use. Or they may make it legal for any use.

But legalizing marijuana may not be the end of the story. States' health boards can severely limit the new law. This happened in Oklahoma in 2018. The health board

Marijuana dispensaries are regulated by the state. Each state can have different rules.

made new rules. It said each **dispensary**

had to have a pharmacist. It also limited

how marijuana could be used. The board

limited the THC levels that would be legal,

too. Marijuana was legal there. But these

restrictions made it harder to get. The regulations were later changed.

WHERE IT'S LEGAL

By early 2019, thirty-three states had legalized some use. This included both medical and **recreational** use. These states were still in the early stages of their new laws. Colorado and Washington developed strong marijuana industries. The states collected taxes from marijuana sales. The money was used to pay for health care. It also paid for addiction treatment.

Some people who want to legalize marijuana say the drug is no more harmful

IN FAVOR OF REGULATION AND RESEARCH

Raphael Mechoulam is a chemist. He researches marijuana. He thinks it should be legalized for medical use. Then it could be strictly regulated. Researchers could study it. "We have just scratched the surface," Mechoulam explains, "and I greatly regret that I don't have another lifetime to devote to this field."

Quoted in Hampton Sides, "Science Seeks to Unlock Marijuana's Secrets," National Geographic, *June 2015. www.nationalgeographic.com.*

than alcohol. But studies point out the damage it can do to teen brains. More research is needed. Scientists may discover new benefits or harms of marijuana use.

There is still a lot that scientists don't know about marijuana.

GLOSSARY

addiction

dependence on a substance, thing, or activity

bronchitis

a swelling in the passages that bring air to the lungs

decriminalizing

changing the status of an act from illegal to legal

dispensary

a store that sells marijuana legally

recreational

something done for fun and not for any kind of work

strains

a part of a group with common ancestry

tolerance

ability to endure a substance

withdrawal

the process of stopping taking a drug

SOURCE NOTES

INTRODUCTION: THE FIRST TIME

1. Quoted in "Stories by Teens," *Marijuana Anonymous*, June 1998. www.marijuana-anonymous.org.

2. Quoted in "Stories by Teens."

3. Quoted in "Stories by Teens."

CHAPTER ONE: WHAT IS MARIJUANA, AND HOW IS IT MADE?

4. Quoted in "Marijuana Worse for Teen Brains than Alcohol, Study Finds," *NBC News*, October 3, 2018. www.nbcnews.com.

5. "Marijuana and Lung Health," *American Lung Association*, March 23, 2015. www.lung.org.

CHAPTER THREE: HOW DOES MARIJUANA USE AFFECT PEOPLE'S LIVES?

6. Judith Grisel, "Pot Holes: Legalizing Marijuana Is Fine. But Don't Ignore the Science on Its Dangers," *Washington Post*, May 25, 2018. www.washingtonpost.com.

FOR FURTHER RESEARCH

BOOKS

Daniel Benjamin, *Marijuana*. Tarrytown, New York: Marshall Cavendish Benchmark, 2012.

Carla Mooney, *The Dangers of Marijuana*. San Diego, CA: ReferencePoint Press, 2017.

Marne Ventura, *The Debate about Legalizing Marijuana*. Lake Elmo, MN: Focus Readers, 2018.

INTERNET SOURCES

"Marijuana," *KidsHealth*, May 2018. https://kidshealth.org

"Marijuana: Facts about Cannabis," *LiveScience*, May 18, 2017. https://www.livescience.com

"The Science of Marijuana: How THC Affects the Brain," *Scholastic*, 2011. http://headsup.scholastic.com

WEBSITES

Behavioral Health Treatment Services Locator
www.findtreatment.samhsa.gov

This website provides information on who to call in a crisis situation.

Marijuana: Facts for Teens, National Institute on Drug Abuse
www.drugabuse.gov

This site, geared toward teens, provides facts about marijuana and other drugs, answers frequently asked questions about the drug, and lists additional resources that may be helpful.

National Institute on Drug Abuse for Teens: Marijuana
https://teens.drugabuse.gov

This site includes information about marijuana and how it affects the body, as well as video games and blog posts geared toward teen readers.

IMAGE CREDITS

ABOUT THE AUTHOR

Kari A. Cornell is a writer and an editor who likes to cook, craft, and tinker in the garden. She has written many books for young readers, including *The Nitty Gritty Gardening Book*, *Dig In: 12 Easy Gardening Projects Using Kitchen Scraps*, and *The Craft-a-Day Book*.